STANDING TOGETHER

PHOTOGRAPHS FROM THE DAILY NEWS

DAILY NEWS

ADMINISTRATION

PRESIDENT:
LES GOODSTEIN

SENIOR VICE PRESIDENT, STRATEGIC MARKETING:
MARIE DEPARIS

EDITORIAL

EDITOR-IN-CHIEF:
EDWARD KOSNER

EXECUTIVE EDITOR:
MICHAEL GOODWIN

DIRECTOR OF PHOTOGRAPHY:
ERIC MESKAUSKAS

DEPUTY DIRECTOR OF PHOTOGRAPHY:
MICHAEL LIPACK

SP L.L.C.

PUBLISHER:
PETER L. BANNON

SENIOR MANAGING EDITORS:
JOSEPH J. BANNON JR. AND SUSAN M. MOYER

ART DIRECTOR:
K. JEFFREY HIGGERSON

SENIOR GRAPHIC DESIGNER:
KENNETH J. O'BRIEN

COORDINATING EDITOR:
ERIN M. LINDEN-LEVY

COPY EDITOR:
CYNTHIA L. MCNEW

ISBN 1-58261-556-x
Printed in Canada

Mike Albans

Contents

Howard Simmons

President's Note

This book is a well-meaning effort to record, for the ages, the horror of the attack on the World Trade Center, zero in on its defining moments and, to the degree possible, lend a measure of historical perspective.

The *Daily News*—photographers, reporters and editors—was well qualified to produce this book. We were on top of the attack almost from the moments of impact. And because it was our responsibility to do so, we have compiled a powerful collection of photographs and words that we believe captures the essence of 9/11.

From the collapse of the twin towers of concrete and steel to the rise of the twin towers of blue light that served as a tribute to those lost, our editors have done their best to select the most defining moments for this book.

It is our solemn hope that, in some small way, the book sends a message to the whole world that the indomitable spirit of New Yorkers and other Americans can't be broken by terrorists, no matter how heinous their attack.

Les Goodstein
President

Keith Bedford

9.11

Smoke billows from the twin towers of the World Trade Center—the aftermath of a terrorist attack. A hijacked American Airlines Boeing 767, originating from Boston's Logan Airport, struck 1 World Trade Center (north tower) at 8:46 a.m. At 9:03 a.m., a United Airlines 767, also hijacked in Boston, crashed into 2 World Trade Center (south tower). Both towers later collapsed.
Susan Watts

People flee to safety following the attacks on Sept. 11. Auto travel was impossible, forcing people to flee on foot away from the devastation.
(left) *Budd Williams* , (above) *Susan Watts*

BY CORKY SIEMASZKO

The first plane hit the north tower at 8:46 a.m. The second crashed into the south tower at 9:03 a.m.

New York is still recovering from the blue-sky morning of Sept. 11 when hijackers sent two jetliners crashing into New York City's mightiest towers.

When the first plane hit, the throngs on the ground stared up at the burning hole in the side of 1 World Trade Center and rubbed their eyes in disbelief. It had to be an accident.

Inside, thousands of workers raced down thousands of stairs to get away. As sirens across the city wailed, the public address system in neighboring 2 World Trade Center urged calm. "Tower 2 is secure," it said.

Then the second plane pierced the south tower's steel skin like a bullet and shattered any illusions that this catastrophe was not part of some sick plan.

The Federal Aviation Administration ordered the skies closed, and President Bush declared New York City under attack by terrorists. Minutes later, a third hijacked plane plowed into the Pentagon and claimed more innocent lives.

Hundreds of cops and firefighters called to the chaos at the Trade Center fought their way through the escaping crowds to get to those still caught inside.

But before they could get everyone out the south tower collapsed, burying rescuers with those they had tried to save.

Falling concrete and steel sent up angry clouds of death and destruction that banished the sun and devoured those who could not escape the narrow canyons in time.

Then the north tower fell, taking with it hundreds more lives. The horror mounted and mounted and mounted.

Firefighters screamed their trapped brothers' names and bloodied their hands trying to reach them in

the rubble. Dazed survivors roamed like ghosts through the streets littered with crushed cars.

Mayor Giuliani, who barely escaped being crushed by the falling towers, shut the city down moments after learning that a fourth hijacked plane bound for Los Angeles crashed in a Pennsylvania field.

"I have a sense it's a horrendous number of lives lost," Giuliani said, the dust from the towers covering his shoulders.

He had never been more right in his life.

Smoke and flames erupt from
a gaping hole in the WTC,
caused by an airplane tearing
through it.
Susan Watts

ABOVE:
A police officer helps a distraught woman as ash and debris cover them both near the site of the WTC terrorist attacks.
Corey Sipkin

BELOW:
What is left of the World Trade Center after the terrorist attacks is a shattered landscape littered with dust and debris.
Thomas Monaster

OPPOSITE:
Large sections of the upper floors of 1 World Trade Center lie in ruins on the ground after it collapsed.
Michael Schwartz

Pat Carroll

Workers Back at It

Workers, some wearing masks against the ash-laden air, line up for identity checks on Nassau St. as they return to their offices for the first time a week after the terrorist attacks.
Linda Rosier

BY CORKY SEISMESKO

By subway, ferry and foot, they returned to lower Manhattan by the thousands.

Battling crowds, mammoth traffic jams and their own fears, the legions of workers who fled after the World Trade Center attacks came back with a vengeance—terrorists be damned.

"It's a bit scary, but I know we have to do this," Joanna Keiser, 37, of Queens, said as she fought her way through the throngs and security checkpoints to get to her law firm. "Just keep going and show we can."

"It's wonderful to be back, to see it open," Mayor Giuliani said before presiding over a meeting with his commissioners. "It's a symbol of New York."

A police officer checks IDs before
allowing workers to enter lower
Manhattan office buildings.
Linda Rosier

Financial District workers wait in
lines around the block to have
their identities checked before
returning to their jobs.
Robert Rosamilio

Evidence of destruction—particularly the pungent gray dust from the pulverized Trade Center—was everywhere. Smoke still billowed from the remnants of 7 World Trade Center.

"It's very sad," said Keith Dunne, 27, an insurance adjuster from Long Beach, L.I. "There are armed guards in Manhattan. Who would have ever thought of a war right in our city?"

Indian immigrant Nilesh Patel also was thinking about security yesterday. He ignored his wife's warning that thugs would mistake him for an Arab. At 10:30 a.m. he reopened his newsstand at Fulton and William Sts.

"We're stuck in last week, frozen in time," Patel, 40, of Queens, said as he surveyed a stack of unsold papers from last Tuesday. "My wife said don't go ... you won't feel safe. But how are we going to survive in this country if we don't work?"

"It's a brand new day," declared 31-year-old Secundino Diaz as he polished a $9,000 watch at the Kenjo store on Wall St. "We are Americans, and Americans don't know when to stop. We just keep going."

And last night, as the evening exodus began, many workers said that while there were moments of chaos and concern, their first day back left them feeling reassured.

The returnees began trickling back before dawn—a few brave souls at a time, some carrying American flags, emerging from subway stations to find a downtown transformed.

Generators hummed at barely lit intersections. Cables snaked through the streets. Flags flew at half-staff. Cops wearing surgical masks manned checkpoints. Crushed cars were stacked atop one another at some corners.

The floor of the New York
Stock Exchange is filled with
traders as Wall Street and the
Financial District get back to
business a week after the
WTC terrorist attacks.
Robert Rosamilio

Grand Central Terminal is uncharacteristically quiet during the morning rush hour as workers return to their jobs in Manhattan for the first time since the terrorist attack.
Susan Watts

Manhattan workers return to their jobs by foot as the Financial District reopens a week after the attacks on the World Trade Center.
Robert Rosamilio

His Words Still Heal Us

Jackie Cannizzaro carries a folded American flag as she walks behind the fire truck carrying the coffin of her husband, Firefighter Brian Cannizzaro, who was killed on Sept. 11.
Debbie Egan-Chin

BY MICHAEL DALY

With heavy hearts, we buried Father Mychal Judge, the Fire Department chaplain whose death certificate bears the number 1, making him the first officially recorded fatality of the World Trade Center attack.

Judge leaves us with words that he uttered in past years at the deaths of John Drennan and Peter McLaughlin and too many other firefighters, words that should help us through all the funerals that are to come.

"My God is a God of surprises," he would say. By that, Judge meant that even the most terrible times present us with wonders.

Judge showed us a wonder of his own when he stepped into mortal danger to administer last rites to a firefighter who had been struck by a woman plummeting from above. He took off his helmet to pray and was hit in the head by debris.

Another wonder came when firefighters then carried him to St. Peter's Church and laid him before the altar, covering him with a white cloth and his priest's stole, laying his helmet and his badge on his chest.

As the wonders burgeoned, celebrity and money paled before bravery and devotion. A movie star was nothing compared to a person laboring on the smoldering mountain of death. The Stars and Stripes appeared everywhere, and the devastation at the tip of Manhattan only made the Statue of Liberty's upraised torch seem to shine brighter.

What a wonder of a funeral it was, with not just the Clintons and Mark Green, but firefighters and even Andrew Brautigan, the 14-month-old grandson of the fallen Fire Capt. John Drennan. His grandmother, Vina Drennan, held the boy as the mourners filled St. Francis of Assisi Church, and she remembered aloud what Judge often said to her after her husband's death seven years ago.

"He used to tell me, 'All is well,'" she said. "And I didn't believe him." She now gazed into Andrew's bright eyes. "All is well," she said.

More smiles came from three of the friars who saw Andrew as they filed up the aisle to escort Judge's remains into the church where he had so often prayed for others. A squad of men in dress blues strode silently past.

When the boy began to fidget, Fire Cap. Michael Currid leaned over from his seat beside Drennan and held out his white uniform hat. The boy hushed, his two tiny hands clutching the hat of the heartbroken man who had so gently placed Judge in a body bag.

33

The Mass commenced and the Rev. Michael Duffy delivered the homily. He recounted how another priest had spotted a plane flying low over Sixth Ave. and had then seen smoke rising from the World Trade Center. The priest had gone straight to Judge, saying, "I think they're going to need you."

Judge had quickly changed from his friar's habit to his chaplain's uniform and dashed off. Word reached Duffy in the afternoon that Judge had been killed.

"I felt my whole spirit fall and turn into a pile of rubble at the bottom of my heart," he recalled.

Duffy said. "We're going to have more and more people brought out of that rubble and Mychal Judge is going to greet them on the other side of death. He's going to greet them with his big Irish smile. He's going to take them by the hand and say, 'Welcome.'"

Among the other speakers was Edward Cardinal Egan, who spoke just as Judge would have. "New York is going to be rebuilt stronger than ever before in the blood and sweat of our heroes," he said.

A close friend, Peter Johnson, also spoke, invoking the words that Judge would have uttered on seeing surprising wonders in a grief-struck city united as one against evil. "How marvelous!"

OPPOSITE:
Firefighter Frederick III 3rd salutes as his mother, Mary, comforts daughter Jennifer after the funeral service for his father at St. Margaret of Antioch Church in Pearl River, Rockland County. Fred III Jr., the 49-year-old captain of Ladder Co. 2, died in the Sept. 11 terrorist attacks.
Chet Gordon

ABOVE:
A police officer with a folded American flag stands beside Theresa Russo and her son Michael Jr. as they pay respects to her husband, Lt. Michael Russo, during a memorial service for the fallen firefighter.
Dennis Clark

Firefighters, with agony
etched on their faces, give a
last salute to their beloved
colleague, the Rev. Mychal
Judge, during his funeral at St.
Francis of Assisi Church on
West 31st Street.
Linda Rosier

Thousands of mourners attended the funeral for Chief of Department Peter Ganci at St. Kilian's Catholic Church in Farmingdale, L.I.
John Roca

FDNY Battalion Chief Raymond Downey's grandson, Peter Tortorici, 5, wears his grandfather's hat and wipes a tear from his eye at a memorial service for Downey.
Willie Anderson

The flag flies high as firefighters line the street during a memorial service for Fire Capt. Vincent Brunton at Holy Name Church on Prospect Park West in Brooklyn.
Todd Maisel

Battlefield Bravest Promoted

Mayor Giuliani embraces a firefighter during a promotion ceremony at the Fire Department headquarters in downtown Brooklyn. One hundred sixty-eight of the city's Bravest were promoted to the officers' ranks to step in for those killed in the World Trade Center tragedy.
Ron Antonelli

BY MICHELE MCPHEE

With red-rimmed eyes, bruised bodies and wounded spirits, 168 of the city's Bravest were elevated to officer ranks in what Mayor Giuliani called "battlefield" promotions to step in for those lost in the World Trade Center collapse.

, the first large casualties are being
by the Fire Department of New York
ani told the firefighters outside FDNY
s in Brooklyn.

ork City Fire Department is being re-
y. It reminds me of battlefield commis-
the time of war," the mayor added.
move forward in memory of those
y have taken some of our most pre-
ut they have not taken our spirit."

ny was held outside under a clear sky
sun, yet it was unusually solemn.

refighters wiped at tears and traded

harrowing stories about where they were when the
twin towers fell.

Many sported ugly welts, yellowing bruises and
deep scratches suffered while digging through the
wreckage for victims. Teary family members flew
American flags from baby carriages and pinned red,
white and blue ribbons on their breasts. High-
ranking fire chiefs wept and hugged.

"It's bittersweet," said Vito Berretta of Ladder Co.
119, who was promoted from firefighter to lieutenant. "It's hard to enjoy this when there are so many
of our brothers still missing."

Fire Commissioner Thomas Von Essen wept and his shoulders trembled as he asked surviving firefighters to stand in for five of the honorees, Deputy Chief Charles Kasper, Battalion Capts. Thomas Haskell and Jimmy Amato, and Lts. Vernon Richards and John Fisher. All five are among the 315 firefighters who are missing.

"We need you to help us attempt to recover the rest of our men that are missing," Von Essen told his men. "We are shaken, but we are not defeated. We stare adversity in the eye, and we push on. That's exactly what we have done in the past, and that's exactly what you will do tomorrow."

His voice shaking, the commissioner added: "I need you guys to go out there and do the very best we can to get our guys out."

Von Essen named 32-year FDNY veteran Daniel Nigro to the post of chief of department, the second in command. Nigro replaced his close friend, Peter Ganci, who died in the collapse.

Deputy Chief Salvatore Cassano was promoted to chief of operations, Nigro's former position.

"This department displayed to the world our resolve to protect everyone in this great city," Nigro told the audience. "It's not easy to get up off the mat after such a blow, but the Fire Department has gotten up."

ABOVE:
Pipers accompany a fire truck bearing the flag-covered coffin of Firefighter James Coyle, 26, of Ladder Co. 3 in Manhattan, who rushed to the World Trade Center on Sept. 11 even though he was on vacation.
Todd Maisel

LEFT:
The flag-covered coffin of FDNY Battalion Chief Raymond Downey rides atop a fire engine during his memorial service.
Bill Turnbull

Others at the ceremony were Sen. Chuck Schumer (D-N.Y.), who said the Fire Department could not be defeated despite the devastating toll of the terrorist attack.

"Today we show that evil man in the mountains across the world that he cannot stop us. With every brave firefighter he took from us, there is another to take his place," Schumer said. "And if, God forbid, they should fall in the line of duty, there will be another behind him and another behind him."

At the benediction that opened the ceremony, the Rev. John Delendick, a Fire Department chaplain, quoted his fallen comrade, the Rev. Mychal Judge, killed as he administered to a fallen firefighter.

"I think [Judge] would say to all of us today as he said to us many times," Delendick said, "'Don't worry about doing this work. You're going to be great, you're going to be fine, because God is with you.'"

Newly appointed Deputy Chief Thomas Jenser, who lost 10 men from his Battalion 8, said the promotions did renew his resolve.

"We lost a lot of really good guys, and it will hurt for a long time," Jenser said. "But this is the New York City Fire Department. We fight back."

ORT AUTHORITY
W YORK & NEW J

Bill Turnbull

Fate of Four Battle-Worn WTC Flags

Capt. Michael Dugan hangs an American flag from a light pole in front of the crumbling World Trade Center.
Andrew Savulich

BY GREG GITTRICH

In the blaze of patriotism sparked by the Sept. 11 attacks, four battle-tested banners stand out for a revered reason: They flew above or were found buried in the rubble of the World Trade Center.

Of the four flags, one now hangs from the *Theodore Roosevelt*, which is leading U.S. warships in the war on terrorism; another was marched into the Olympics after flying at memorial services for several slain cops; a third escaped destruction and appears destined for the Smithsonian Institution, and the final looks to be lost forever.

"The flag is a rallying point," Capt. Richard O'Hanlon, commanding officer of the *Roosevelt*, told the *Daily News* from the north Arabian Sea.

"[The flag] is a silent message of inspiration not only to us but to all Americans that we will be victorious, we will not falter and we will go on to enjoy the freedoms we so cherish."

The banner on the *Roosevelt* is perhaps the most well-known of the four Ground Zero flags. It was raised atop the Trade Center rubble by three firefighters, a solemn moment captured by photographer Tom Franklin.

On Sept. 23, Gov. Pataki and former Mayor Rudy Giuliani signed the flag and sent it to the *Roosevelt*. It has flown over 12 battleships in the fleet.

The only flag that was flying atop the Trade Center on Sept. 11—the second of the Ground Zero

banners—was buried in debris for three days. Rescuers handed it over to a National Guard colonel for a ceremonial destruction, but the colonel passed it along to its owner, the Port Authority, which lost 37 police officers in the attack.

The delicate banner, torn in two places, is stored in a triangular wooden container and only unfurled for special ceremonies. It has flown at all the memorials for the fallen Port Authority cops, the World Series, the Super Bowl and the city's Veterans Day and Thanksgiving Day parades.

"Anyone who lays an eye on this remnant of Sept. 11 is hard-pressed not to be moved by it," said Pasquale DiFulco, a Port Authority spokesman. "At the Olympics, 55,000 people fell silent when it was presented before the national anthem."

The final resting place of the banner has yet to be determined. But one thing is for sure, it won't be burned—a fate narrowly escaped by the third Ground Zero flag, which fell from an upper floor of one of the twin towers.

Pulled from the searing rubble by an unidentified federal agent, the banner was covered in ash and missing 12 stars. The agent turned the sullied flag over to an American Legion post in New Providence, N.J.

A third of the banner was torn away and the veterans group planned to incinerate the rest. The decision was in line with a 1923 congressional mandate, but it outraged some people.

The veterans compromised, cut about 6 inches off the flag and burned the swatch. The banner was then given to the FBI. The Smithsonian's National Museum of American History is talking with the FBI about obtaining the flag.

The final of the four Ground Zero flags is missing and feared destroyed.

On Sept. 11, FDNY Capt. Michael Dugan raised the Stars and Stripes from a light pole in front of the fallen Trade Center. "When I saw that flag I said we've got to get it up," recalled Dugan, whose act was photographed by the *Daily News*.

"As soon as we got it up, they told us to get out of the area—another building was going to fall. I have no idea what happened to the flag. No one has seen it since."

A lone American flag waves in the smoke on Liberty St., overlooking the debris of the World Trade Center.
Michael Schwartz

Todd Maisel

Newly Beloved, Mayor Basks In City's Farewell

Outgoing Mayor Rudy Giuliani shakes hands with an audience member as he walks up the aisle of St. Paul's Chapel on Broadway to give his final speech before his term ends.
Susan Watts

BY DAVID SALTONSTALL

It was French President Jacques Chirac who memorably dubbed Mayor Giuliani "Rudy the Rock" in the days after Sept. 11. But to anyone who has watched Giuliani walk the city's streets recently, Rudy the Rock Star may be more like it.

Women swoon. Men's jaws go momentarily slack. Hands thrust forward. And in the mayor's wake he inevitably leaves behind raucous ovations of "RU-DY, RU-DY" or, just as often, a stream of whispered "God-bless-yous" and other thanks.

"It's a little like Superman walking through your door," said John Ivanac, manager of the Trio Restaurant, after Giuliani popped in for dinner at the E. 33rd St. bistro this month. "Pretty much everyone in the place stood up and gave him this rousing ovation. We had a musician on hand who started playing 'New York, New York,' and everyone started singing," added Ivanac. "It gave you chills."

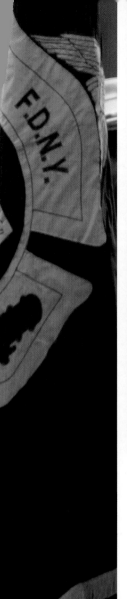

Mayor Giuliani speaks at St. Vincent's Medical Center the day after the terrorist attacks as City Council Speaker Peter Vallone (left) and Fire Commissioner Thomas Von Essen look on.
Kristen Artz

Fire Commissioner Thomas Von Essen and Mayor Giuliani stand side by side in St. Patrick's Cathedral during a memorial service for Donald Burns, assistant chief of the Fire Department.
Susan Watts

Clearly, Giuliani is a mayor who went out on top, propelled by the deep emotional currents that still flow from his handling of the World Trade Center attacks. His image has moved beyond local politics and into the realm of national, and even international, celebrity.

It's a farewell that most mayors never get in New York.

For Giuliani, who at times during his often contentious administration was more likely to be met with stony silence, if not outright jeers when he walked the streets, these are clearly days to savor.

"I much prefer this to everybody disliking me," he deadpanned as he strolled along 57th St., greeting throngs of well-wishers. "It's a wonderful feeling. I feel like all the hard work we did ... is appreciated, and it's great. It's really great.

"It is the source of a lot of strength," Giuliani said of the cheers and thumbs-up. "And then a lot of people will come up to me and say, 'I came to New York because you asked me to come.'"

As Giuliani continued his march along 57th St., which was jammed with the usual throngs of shoppers and tourists, he shook hands with anyone who extended an arm. He posed with babies. He kissed the ring of a 50-year-old woman who spoke to him in Italian. And anyone from out of town got a hearty thanks. "You visiting?" he asked one couple from Richmond, Va. "Good. Spend lots of money."

Then it was on to another handshake, another hug, another picture. As the mayor walked an elderly African-American woman across the street at 58th St., she turned to him and said, "I've been very impressed [since Sept. 11]. You been holding out on us."

Their shopping done, Giuliani and girlfriend Judith Nathan dashed across the street for a bite of frozen yogurt at the World of Nuts & Ice Cream shop, where the manager insisted on treating.

"No, if I don't pay I'll be in deep trouble," said the mayor, drawing out his wallet.

Giuliani and Nathan then made a beeline for a waiting car. But before they sped away, the mayor turned and raised his tiny cup of yogurt in the air, as if in a toast to the 30 or so gawkers who huddled on the narrow sidewalk. The crowd erupted in applause.

"We love you," screamed one woman.

In two months, he was knighted by the queen of England. He has been serenaded by Tony Bennett, Natalie Cole and Bette Midler at a celebrity tribute. His endorsement of Mayor-elect Michael Bloomberg is widely credited with having kept City Hall in Republican hands for an unprecedented third term in a row.

And he appeared on *Saturday Night Live*, for the fourth time on the show as mayor. In the "Week-end Update" segment, cast member Tina Fey thanked Giuliani for holding the city together. The mayor joined Fey and co-anchor Jimmy Fallon in a

warm if off-key rendition of "Will You Love Me Tomorrow."

"Both the interaction with the crowds and then dealing with the families of the firefighters and police officers who died, going to the memorial services," said Giuliani. "It gives you a great deal of strength.

"You see that the human spirit has survived the worst attack that anyone could have imagined," he said. "And is maybe in a certain sense even strengthened by it."

What ties us together? We're tied together by our belief in political democracy. We're tied together by our belief in religious freedom. We're tied together by our belief in capitalism, a free economy where people make their own choices about the spending of their money. We're tied together because we respect human life. We're tied together because we respect the rule of law. Those are the group of ideas that make us Americans.

We are an open city. We have never been afraid of people. We've never been afraid of people no matter what their color, religion, ethnic background. We're a city in which our diversity is our greatest strength.

Long after we are all gone, it's the sacrifice of our patriots and their heroism that is going to be what this place is remembered for. This is going to be a place that is remembered 100 and 1,000 years from now, like the great battlefields of Europe and of the United States.

—excerpts from former Mayor Giuliani's December 27, 2001 farewell speech

ABOVE:
Outgoing Mayor Giuliani gives his final speech at St. Paul's Chapel on Broadway.
Susan Watts

OPPOSITE:
Israeli Prime Minister Ariel Sharon (left) and Mayor Giuliani talk as they look out over the site of the destroyed World Trade Center.
Susan Watts

Harry Hamburg

Morning Like Sept. 11

Rescue workers silently gaze
at a steel cross recovered
from the rubble of the World
Trade Center and remember
their comrades at a ceremony
marking six months since the
Sept. 11 terrorist attacks.
Todd Maisel

BY GREG GITTRICH, DAVID SALTONSTALL AND CORKY SIEMASZKO

When dawn broke on the day New York remembered its dead, the sky was nearly as blue as on the morning when two hijacked planes brought down Manhattan's tallest towers.

But it was bitter cold in the depths of Ground Zero, where cops and construction workers were collecting victims' remains in the northern end of the site.

Just before 8:46 a.m., the time when the first of the hijacked planes crashed into the north tower, a deep voice crackled over the public address system: "All members, we will now observe a moment of silence."

Port Authority Police Officer Anthony Croce, who helped scores of people escape the north tower, put down his shovel and took off his hardhat. The construction workers did the same. And for a minute, silence reigned in the pit.

"This is where I want to be," Croce said. "I didn't die by the grace of God. Now I want to help families by finding the people who didn't make it."

A few blocks from the ruins, dignitaries and grieving relatives carrying yellow daffodils and photos of those they lost gathered at Battery Park for another ceremony.

They huddled against a brisk wind around "The Sphere," a steel and bronze sculpture that had

stood in the fountain of the Trade Center plaza and was gashed by falling debris.

Bloomberg's predecessor, Rudy Giuliani, urged mourners to look to the victims "for our inspiration and our sense of purpose. They would want us to lift up our heads very, very high."

Edwin Morales, who lost his cousin Ruben Correa, a firefighter, fought back tears. "I know some people say this is too hard, but this is something I need," he said. "I need to be here."

So did Charles Wolf, who lost his wife, Katherine.

"Every one of us remembers our loved ones in our heart every single day," Wolf said. "But once in a

while you do something like this as a public remembrance to make sure that we know that the city, the government and the people still care."

The ceremony ended when a firefighter rang four sets of five bell rings—the traditional signal for a fallen firefighter.

Trading on the New York Stock Exchange usually begins at 9:30 a.m., but traders who arrived there early fell silent at 8:46 and again at 9:03—the time the second plane hit—to honor the dead.

At nearby St. Paul's Chapel, the names of the attack victims from the Trade Center, the Pentagon and the plane crash in Pennsylvania were read aloud.

At police stationhouses around the city, the names of the 23 cops killed in the terror attack were read aloud.

"Police Officer James Leahy, 6th Precinct; Police Officer Robert Fazio, 13th Precinct," Capt. David Barrere said as he read the names to two dozen officers standing at attention outside the 76th Precinct stationhouse in Carroll Gardens, Brooklyn.

"They were called on to act and did so with the highest valor," Barrere said after he finished the list, which ended with "Detective Claude Richards, bomb squad."

In Rubble,
a Sacred Find

BY GREG GITTRICH AND
CORKY SIEMASZKO

When the World Trade Center collapsed, a section of the steel girders that supported the mighty north tower landed in the rubble in the shape of a cross. Since that terrible day, the cross has become an inspiration to many of the firefighters and workers at Ground Zero.

"Behold the glory of the cross at Ground Zero," the Rev. Brian Jordan, a Franciscan priest, said as he sprinkled holy water on the steel during a blessing ceremony. "This is our symbol of hope, our symbol of faith, our symbol of healing."

The cross was found by laborer Frank Silecchia. He said he found the cross standing almost completely upright, two days after the towers fell. "Some people will say it's velocity or physics that put it there," Silecchia said. "To me, it's an act of God."

The Rev. Brian Jordan leads a prayer at the dedication of the cross-shaped steel girders found in the WTC rubble.
Michael Schwartz

Kristen Artz

2 Towers of Light Rise in Tribute to WTC Lost

Red roses, left at the foot of
the Tribute in Light, a
temporary memorial to the
victims of the World Trade
Center disaster. The twin
columns of light illuminated
the skyline for one month
beginning on March 11, 2002,
the six-month anniversary of
the attacks.
James Keivom

BY GREG GITTRICH, DAVID SALTONSTALL AND CORKY SEISMESKO

Twin beacons of light evoking the lost World Trade Center split the night sky on March 11—reaching to the stars and capping a day of prayers and remembrances for the victims of Sept. 11.

Generated by 88 powerful spotlights, shafts of light that could be seen by astronauts aboard the international space station rose up from Ground Zero and filled the yawning gap in the skyline.

"This is the light that shines up on our brothers in heaven," said Firefighter Van Johnson, 50, of Ladder 124 in Bushwick, Brooklyn. "Or better yet, this is the light that they are shining down on us."

Mayor Bloomberg said the lights are temporary memorials for the nearly 3,000 people who perished. "The real memorial will be in our hearts," Bloomberg said.

The lights were turned on by 12-year-old Valerie Webb, whose father, Port Authority Police Officer Nathaniel Webb, was killed Sept. 11.

And as opera star Jessye Norman sang "America the Beautiful," her soaring soprano echoing across the 16-acre site, construction workers were moved to tears. "I come down here to do the work, but I also think of what really took place here, and it is devastating," said electrician Daniel Marcinkowski, 38, of Lyndhurst, N.J.

Let There Be Lights

DAILY NEWS EDITORIAL

They stood in the blustery winds for hours at Ground Zero. They gathered on rooftops in Manhattan, along the waterfront in Brooklyn and on the Palisades in New Jersey. Miles to the west, they hiked up a mountain to a cliff with a view of the skyline. They created traffic jams in towns along the Hudson, and on the highways heading toward the city.

Six months after their lives were darkened by a black cloud of smoke and sorrow and shock, the people of New York—and New Jersey—were again gazing skyward. This time, with hope. And a renewal of resolve. Two towers of light, rising above Ground Zero, cast their glory into the night. And rising with them, as on angels' wings, were countless loving prayers for the lost.

It was as if a wound had healed. That great empty place in the lower Manhattan skyscape was filled once again. Said Firefighter Van Johnson of Ladder 124, "This is the light that shines up on our brothers in heaven. Or better yet, this is the light that they are shining down on us." Our Bravest, it seems, are also our poet laureates.

The lights shining up and down glow in tribute to all the brothers, and sisters, and fathers, and mothers, and sons and daughters who perished Sept. 11. These people will live within us forever.

ABOVE:
Crowds gather to watch as the Tribute in Light beams into the sky from Ground Zero on its final night. The twin columns of light, which have shone until 11 p.m. since the six-month anniversary of the attack, will be left on all night as a grand finale before being extinguished at dawn.
James Keivom

OPPOSITE:
The Tribute in Light rises skyward for the first time, six months after the terrorist attacks. The lighting ceremony capped a day of prayers and remembrance for the victims of Sept. 11. At right are the lights of the Brooklyn Bridge, across the East River.
Todd Maisel

88 individual 7,000-watt xenon arc tubes shine together to form the Tribute in Light, a temporary memorial at Ground Zero.
James Keivom

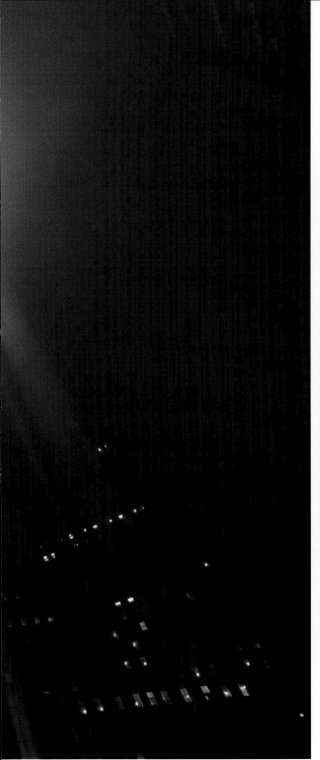

LEFT:
Firefighters John Leimeister (left) and Sean MacPherson look up at beams cast by searchlights making up the Tribute in Light, no doubt remembering their lost comrades.
Michael Appleton

ABOVE:
Lighting technicians Michelle Dumitriu (left) and Ray Preziosi adjust the equipment which will beam two towering columns of light into the night sky at the site of the destroyed World Trade Center six months after the tragedy.
Keith Bedford

White House Ceremony For WTC Kin

An honor guard stands in
front of the Capitol building
during a ceremony honoring
fallen police officers.
Harry Hamburg

BY BY KENNETH R. BAZINET IN WASHINGTON AND EMILY GEST IN NEW YORK

Jennie Farrell feels she just has to be at the White House today.

"That's where I really want to be," said Farrell, 39, of Wantagh, L.I., who lost her 26-year-old brother, James, an electrician, in the World Trade Center's Tower 2 on Sept. 11. "I live that day; it's etched in my heart forever."

Farrell—along with 300 family members who lost relatives in September's terrorist attacks on the World Trade Center, the Pentagon and aboard Flight 93—will gather on the South Lawn of the White House this morning for a ceremony with President Bush.

"The families represent the magnitude of what was done on Sept. 11 to our country," Farrell said. "It should be about them always."

She will attend the ceremony with her husband, Daniel, and their 9-year-old son, who is named after his uncle James.

After a service featuring the Boys Choir of Harlem, Bush will deliver what is being billed as another in a series of major speeches aimed at renewing the call for a lasting war on terror.

At the Pentagon's six-month commemoration, Defense Secretary Donald Rumsfeld will welcome military leaders from Central Command and representatives of coalition allies who joined the U.S. in the war on terrorism.

In a separate Pentagon ceremony, some 700 Jewish leaders from around the world will join military and political officials at 9:38 a.m., the moment when the third hijacked airliner crashed into the Pentagon.

President Bush greets youngsters at a White House ceremony honoring police officers who died in the line of duty. Special attention was given to those officers who died during the Sept. 11 attacks.

Harry Hamburg

The President speaks at a ceremony at the Capitol, praising the heroics of the police during the attacks on America and honoring those who died in the line of duty.

Harry Hamburg

PA Bells Toll for Flight 93 Victims

The mournful peal of church bells filled the air in Shanksville, Pa. as hundreds crammed into a small church to honor the heroes of United Airlines Flight 93. Residents and relatives first joined together in a moment of silence at 10:06 a.m., the moment the hijacked flight plunged from the sky six months prior and crashed into a lonely field 2 miles away.

As a clergyman at the Shanksville United Methodist Church read the names of the 40 passengers and crew who died, church bells across the countryside tolled once for each victim.

Church pastor the Rev. Ronald Emery said the attacks have brought America together. "What started as a knot in our stomach as pain and hurt has become the thread that holds us together," Emery said. "Flight 93 is that scarlet thread."

Marcy Nackie, whose brother-in-law Louis Nackie died in the crash, said the spot should be a national memorial. "This is hallowed ground," she said. "This is where the first battle in the war on terrorism happened. It was the Battle of Shanksville."

The inscription on the bronze marker reads, "This memorial is in memory of the brave men and women who gave their lives to save so many others. Their courage and love of our country will be a source of strength and comfort to our great nation."

September the 11th was not the beginning of global terror, but it was the beginning of the world's concerted response. History will know that day not only as a day of tragedy, but as a day of decision — when the civilized world was stirred to anger and to action.

More dangers and sacrifices lie ahead. Yet, America is prepared. Our resolve has only grown, because we remember. We remember the horror and heroism of that morning — the death of children on a field trip, the resistance of passengers on a doomed airplane, the courage of rescuers who died with strangers they were trying to save.

Every nation should know that, for America, the war on terror is not just a policy, it's a pledge. I will not relent in this struggle for the freedom and security of my country and the civilized world.

Together, we will face the peril of our moment, and seize the promise of our times.

—excerpts from President Bush's speech on March 11, 2002

With the flags of many nations behind him, President Bush takes part in a ceremony in memory of those who died in the Sept. 11 terrorist attacks. Ambassadors and dignitaries joined victims' family members on the White House South Lawn for the memorial.
Harry Hamburg

Ron Antonelli

Firefighters carry a black and purple banner emblazoned with the number of Bravest lost on Sept. 11 as they lead a group of 343 firefighters, each marching for one of their slain comrades, along Fifth Ave. in the 241st annual St. Patrick's Day parade.
Mike Albans

343 Bravest Stand Up For 343 Gallant Souls

ABOVE:
Somber New York City firefighters carry photographs of their fallen
brothers as they march past St. Patrick's Cathedral on Fifth Ave. during
the parade. Police and firefighters got the loudest cheers and endless
applause as one of the largest crowds ever came out to celebrate and
remember those lost in the terror attacks.
Linda Rosier

OPPOSITE:
The sound of skirling bagpipes fills the air as piper Tom Gerondel of the
Fire Department Emerald Society Pipe Band provides a tune to march to
at the Throgs Neck St. Patrick's Day Parade in the Bronx.
Michael Schwartz

BY MICHAEL DALY

The pipe band went silent, the crowd hushed and Fifth Ave. became quieter than a whis-pered prayer as the 343 firefighters turned about face toward the place where 343 comrades had perished.

"Uncover!" a voice called out.

The firefighters removed their hats and stood with the wind at their backs. The air itself seemed to gust downtown with their thoughts and memories.

Each of these firefighters was representing a particular member of the department who had died at the World Trade Center. They had joined the formation earlier in the morning on E. 44th St. by speaking the name of a son, brother or friend to a lieutenant from the ceremonial unit who held a list of the dead.

The first to arrive was Firefighter Steve Wall. He gave the name of his best friend. "Matty Ryan."

The lieutenant penciled a check on the list next to Battalion Chief Matthew Ryan. Wall stepped into a 40-by-80-foot section of the block that had been ringed with barricades and marked with a sign reading "Honor Company 343."

"We used to march every year together," Wall said of Ryan. "He was my best friend. ...They found him with two firemen the Saturday night before Thanksgiving."

More firefighters checked in with the lieutenant, Nick Aufiero. Firefighter Michael Stackpole was there to march for his brother, Capt. Timothy Stackpole, who had suffered terrible burns in a fire and then fought his way back to the job only to die on Sept. 11.

Retired Firefighter John Tipping arrived to represent the son also named John whose remains he had helped carry from the Trade Center just last Tuesday. He spoke with Fire Chaplain Christopher Keenan, who was there to march for Fire Chaplain Mychal Judge.

"Did John have a family?" Keenan asked.

"He was just going to get married," Tipping said, walking over to several firefighters from his son's company, Ladder Co. 4. "These are my boys now," Tipping said.

Capt. Danny Browne of Ladder Co. 3 went up to Aufiero with his own list of the 12 from his company who had perished and those who would

be marching for them. The number happened to match the march formation. "Each row is 12, so we have one row," Browne said.

And everywhere you looked, there was more proof of the enormity of losing even one.

Just before noon, the pipe band started onto Fifth Ave., its newest members including James Dowdell, son of the still-missing Lt. Kevin Dowdell. It was followed by 343 probationary firefighters carrying an equal number of flags.

"The future," a firefighter said.

Then came a trio of firefighters bearing a black and purple banner that had the number 343 in white.

Right behind them came the 343 firefighters. The number 12 never looked bigger than when you looked down Ladder Co. 3's row and considered this was how many that firehouse lost.

As all 343 started up Fifth Ave., the biggest St. Patrick's Day crowd any of them had ever seen broke into cheers and applause. A good number of firefighters seemed to be welling with tears even as they smiled.

The cheers seemed to grow even louder as they continued uptown on what had on every other year been just a happy lark up Fifth Ave. They were just below 55th St. when they stopped and turned about with the rest of the parade. The moment of silence deepened to where the only sound was the slap of the ropes against the metal flagpoles overhead.

The roar of the crowd reached the firefighters a little earlier than some might have wished, but there was no mistaking that the moment had come to turn back around. More than one of the 343 had tears on his cheeks as they marched on uptown for 343 gallant souls who were gone but not forgotten on St. Patrick's Day.

Mike Albans

A Final Farewell to Moira

Holding her father's hand, Patricia Smith, 2, leaves the stage wearing the Medal of Honor awarded posthumously to her mother, at the Police Department's annual Medal Day at Carnegie Hall. Officer Moira Smith was one of the 23 officers killed in the Sept. 11 terrorist attack to receive the department's highest award.
(far left) *Susan Watts,*
(left) *Harry Hamburg*

LEFT:
Police Officer Moira Smith leads injured Edward Nicholls, a broker at Aon Corporation, to safety from the burning World Trade Center just before the collapse of the first tower. Officer Smith, who worked at the 13th Precinct, was killed in the disaster minutes after this photograph was taken.
Corey Sipkin

RIGHT:
Patricia Smith salutes as her mother's coffin passes in front of New York's Finest.
Mike Albans

BY PATRICE O'SHAUGHNESSY

The father and his toddler daughter stepped out of the limousine into a biting wind for the funeral. He hoisted the girl up in his arm, dabbed her nose with a tissue and they grinned in the closeness of being two, who once were three.

James Smith never took his eyes off the flag-draped coffin of his wife, Moira, as it was borne into Our Lady of Lourdes Church in Queens Village. But 2 1/2-year-old Patricia stared only at a bagpiper who played "Amazing Grace."

It was a final farewell to Police Officer Moira Smith more than six months after she died helping others escape the hell of the World Trade Center.

Some 300 cops filed out of the cold into the church, and one was reminded of all the people streaming out of the fiery south tower on a late summer day, as Moira Smith calmly ordered the escapees to keep moving out of the lobby, not allowing them to stop to look at the destruction outside, preventing a logjam.

That was after the 38-year-old cop—the only woman from the NYPD to die that day—led a bleeding, dazed insurance executive away from the building, the pair captured in a now-famous *Daily News* photograph.

"Our only real vocation on the face of the earth is that we be loving servants," said the Rev. Al LoPinto. "Moira brought out someone and she could have at that moment said 'I've done my share,' but she returned to see who else she might serve in this terrible moment of calamity."

As the priest spoke of her mother, Patricia played with prayer books and marched back and forth in the pew.

"On that morning, God knew whose shoulder He was tapping when He had her rush to the site," LoPinto said.

"Our girl is home now," James Smith, also a city cop, told the mourners in a shaky voice, "but there are still many more families out there who need our prayers.

"Her most important gift is her final example," he said.

Police Commissioner Raymond Kelly spoke of another photo of Moira Smith from that day, one that James Smith carries in his pocket.

It shows her on 14th St.—the twin towers in the distance behind her, one of them afire—helping witnesses to the attack into a police van.

"She took them to the 13th Precinct, and she could have stayed there to take their statements, but she got a group and headed down there, and she stayed. She just had something special in her. ... This is why people become cops."

Smith was last heard from between the fifth and third floors of the south tower, assisting an asthma patient.

After the funeral, father and daughter walked out of the church to see the hundreds of cops saluting the coffin. Patricia's left hand held her father's, and her right came up to her forehead, as she smiled broadly and mimicked the somber cops.

She kept saluting as her father pulled her near and wrapped his overcoat around her and the coffin was carried away.

117

Ferry Fine
Honor for Hero

BY MICHELE MCPHEE

Two-year-old Patricia Mary Smith promised to buy her mother a boat. But before she could grow up and fulfill her pledge, the little girl's mother died evacuating people from the south tower of the World Trade Center on Sept. 11.

Moira Smith got her boat, in a way, when her husband, James, also a city cop, helped their only daughter christen a NY Waterway ferry named for the fallen heroine.

The christening of the Moira Smith is especially poignant for Jim Smith, a close friend said. The friend recalled the exchange between little Patricia and her parents, when they donated the family's old Winnebago to a children's charity at the end of the summer.

Jim and Moira pretended to cry as the Winnebago was towed away, and their daughter tried to comfort them. "Don't worry, Daddy, I'll buy you a new truck!" she exclaimed. When Moira Smith asked, "What about me?" the girl promised: "I'll buy you a fast boat."

The 64-foot ferry Moira Smith bears the fallen officer's picture, her name in bold black lettering and a plaque that reads, in part: "This ferry is named in honor of Police Officer Moira Smith and her 22 brother New York Police Officers who made the ultimate sacrifice at the World Trade Center September 11, 2001."

MOIRA SMITH

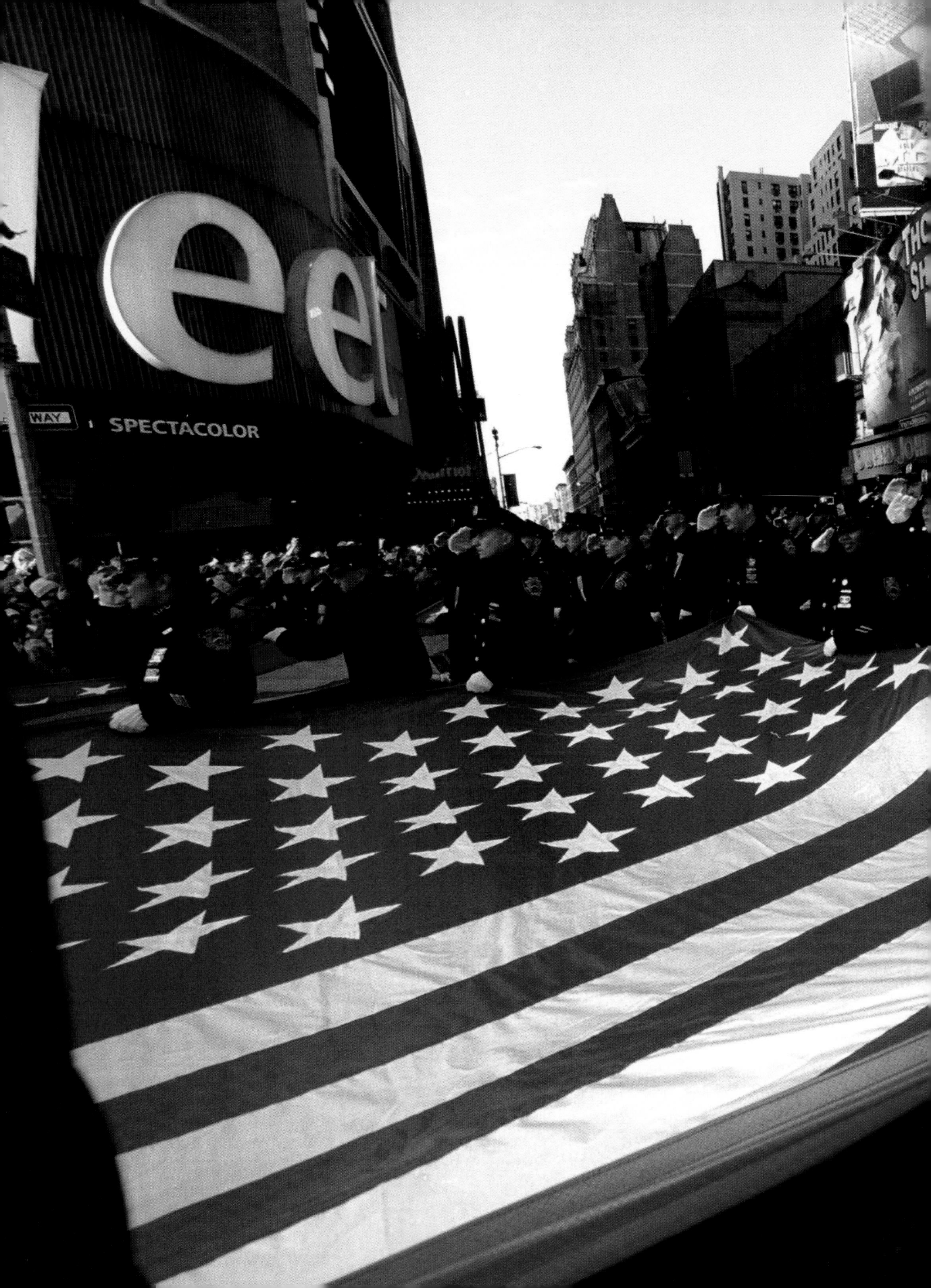
WAY
SPECTACOLOR

To Bravest, He's a 'Regular Guy'

Mayor-elect Michael Bloomberg dons an FDNY cap, a gift from the firefighters of Engine 44, during a Christmas Day visit to the firehouse.
Susan Watts

BY MICHAEL DALY

The story of the painted firehouse began in January, when our billionaire mayor ap-proached three uniformed firefighters who attended a tenants' gathering to accept an award on behalf of their comrades.

Mayor Bloomberg asked the firefighters where they worked and how they were faring. Battalion Chief Richard Burban said he was there representing Ladder Co. 3 in Manhattan.

"Did you lose anybody in the firehouse?" Bloomberg asked.

"We lost 12," Burban said.

ABOVE:
Mayor Bloomberg waves a flag with some young patriots as he joins the Memorial Day Parade on Metropolitan Ave. in Queens.
Todd Maisel

LEFT:
Mayor Bloomberg stands amidst fire officials during funeral of Fire Lt. Kevin Pfeifer at St. Margaret's Church in Middle Village, Queens. Bloomberg eulogized the fallen hero and praised the bravery of all the firefighters who responded to the attacks.
Mike Albans

Bloomberg seemed genuinely concerned. Burban tendered an invitation that was no less genuine, though he did not imagine anything would come of it.

"We're right on 13th St. — if you're ever in the neighborhood, stop by and visit," Burban would remember saying.

"Yes, I'll definitely do that," Bloomberg said.

Bloomberg stepped away and Burban figured the mayor had just been saying what a mayor would say. An aide then appeared and gave Burban her card.

"She told me, 'He really wants to do this,'" Burban recalled. "I was like, 'Wow, that's pretty cool.'"

Later, Burban E-mailed the aide at the address on her card, inviting the mayor to dinner on Super Bowl Sunday. He included his home phone number, and not long afterward the aide called to say the mayor could not make dinner, but would love to come for lunch. "What does he like for lunch?" Burban would remember asking.

"Believe it or not, hot dogs," the aide said. "I kid you not."

On the afternoon of Super Bowl Sunday, Bloomberg arrived as promised at the firehouse just off Union Square. He had on a suit and tie, but he strode in past Ladder 3's new rig with no more airs than if he were wearing a blue work shirt. The old rig had been destroyed down at the World Trade Center.

In the back, Bloomberg was shown a glass case on the wall containing a Ladder 3 ax that had been recovered from the pile. The handle and blade were still covered with the gray ash that triggers too many memories for anybody who was down there. Pictures of the 12 who died were in two rows of six above and below the ax.

Capt. Dan Browne told Bloomberg about each firefighter. The second picture in from the left on the top was the smoke-blackened face of another captain with the same surname, minus the 'e.'

Browne noted that Capt. Patrick Brown had been one of the most decorated firefighters in the history of the department.

The late Capt. Brown gazed from the wall as our present mayor sat down for a chicken parmigiana hero with heroes. Burban did his best to be a good host, asking Bloomberg about his kids. The two joked about raising teenage girls.

At a more serious moment, Bloomberg assured the firefighters that he appreciated what they and the cops had done for the city even before Sept. 11.

"He did say, 'Crime is down. Fires are down. You guys are doing a good job,'" Browne recalled.

Before he left, the mayor toured the firehouse. Browne noted that half the lockers of the fallen firefighters had been left just as they were.

"I wanted him to know the healing process is going to take a long time," Browne later said.

The walls of the locker room were peeling and the whole firehouse was badly in need of painting. Browne said a work order was in, and they hoped

by the first anniversary of Sept. 11 the place would look more like what it truly is, a palace of bravery.

"Why hasn't it been done before?" Bloomberg asked.

Browne noted that the Fire Department had been run on a tight budget even during the boom time.

"I said, 'When you look to make cutbacks, you'll see there's only about four painters for the whole department,'" Browne recalled.

As if to confirm Burban and Browne's good opinion, a painting crew arrived at the firehouse on E. 13th St. The crew got right to work, and the firehouse door was getting a new coat of red paint as Browne offered Bloomberg an unlikely compliment for a billionaire mayor.

"He's a regular guy," Browne said.

Burban joined Browne in saying that from everything they saw, Bloomberg's heart is with the firefighters and therefore in the right place.

"A good regular guy," Burban said.

LEFT:
Mayor Bloomberg salutes during a memorial ceremony outside the Squad 1 firehouse in Park Slope, Brooklyn. Bloomberg placed a wreath to honor the 12 squad members who died in the WTC attack.
Todd Maisel

RIGHT:
Mayor Bloomberg takes the oath of office during his inauguration ceremony on the steps of City Hall.
Linda Rosier

Mayor Bloomberg and Fire Commissioner Nicholas Scoppetta look at a brand new fire truck at Ladder Co. 10. It is the first fire engine delivered to replace those los in the Sept. 11 terrorist attack. The mural on the truck's side shows a firefighter raising the American flag at Ground Zero. *Todd Maisel*

Bush is given WTC megaphone

President Bush, surrounded by rain-soaked rescue workers, waves an American flag from atop a wrecked fire truck in the midst of rubble of what was once the World Trade Center. Bush thanked the workers for their tireless efforts to locate victims.
Harry Hamburg

BY KENNETH R. BAZINET

It's an image the world will never forget: President Bush atop a crumpled fire truck at Ground Zero using a bullhorn to rally the nation after the Sept. 11 terror attack.

Yesterday, he got the bullhorn back.

"It's a historic, really historic memento—something we didn't choose, but it's one of those days that I'll never forget," Bush said, recalling his ad-libbed remarks on Sept. 14.

On that day, retired FDNY Firefighter Bob Beckwith gave Bush the bullhorn to address rescue workers who were chanting "U.S.A.! U.S.A.!"

"I can hear you," Bush yelled to them. "The rest of the world hears you and the people who knocked these buildings down will hear all of us soon."

Gov. Pataki, flanked by Beckwith, handed Bush the bullhorn at a White House ceremony.

Pataki called Bush's remarks at the World Trade Center "incredibly inspirational" to everyone at Ground Zero.

"It turned out to be one of those moments where I had a chance to speak to the world on behalf of the citizens of New York," Bush said as he was given the bullhorn in the Oval Office.

Bush adviser Karen Hughes said Bush's speech was a defining moment in his presidency.

"Somehow in those three sentences, he managed to crystallize the strength and determination of our country and our fierce resolve in the face of this terrible attack," she said.

Beckwith wasn't even supposed to be on the fire truck with Bush.

He said Bush adviser Karl Rove had asked him to "jump up and down" on the fire truck to make sure it was safe.

"He said, 'Somebody is coming over here, and when they get here you help them up and then you come down.'"

But when Bush showed up, the President overruled Rove.

"He said, 'Where you going?' I said, 'I was supposed to get down,'" Beckwith, 69, recalled.

But Bush fired back, "You stay right here," Beckwith said with a grin.

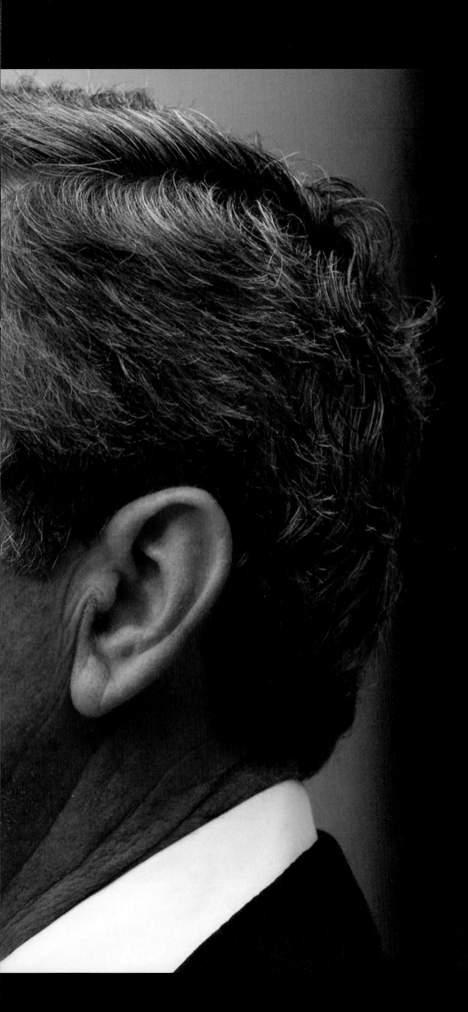

President Bush announces another advance in the war on terrorism—freezing the financial assets of individuals and groups that aid terrorists—as Secretary of State Powell looks on.
Harry Hamburg

LEFT:
President Bush visits Manhattan for the second time since the attack on the World Trade Center to propose an economic stimulus package to aid local businesses in the wake of the attacks.
Mike Albans

RIGHT:
President Bush gives an impassioned plea to other countries to stand with America in the face of terrorism.
Harry Hamburg

Port Authority Police Officer David Lim addresses more than 100 fellow K-9 unit cops during a memorial service at Liberty State Park for his former partner Sirius, a 5-year-old yellow Labrador retriever. Sirius was killed during the Sept. 11 terrorist attacks at the World Trade Center and was the only police dog to die in the attacks.

Sirius was a bomb-sniffing dog for the World Trade Center and was in his kennel in the basement of the tower when it collapsed. His remains were found in January and were removed draped with an American flag. Workers recovered his metal water dish and presented it to Lim at the ceremony.
Heidi Schumann

Final Girder
Taken Down

A crane places the last steel girder from Ground Zero onto a flatbed truck in a ceremony to mark the end of the recovery operation that began after the Sept. 11 terrorist attack on the World Trade Center.
James Keivom

BY GREG GITTRICH AND CORKY SEISMESKO

Now there's nothing left.

Two hundred sixty days after a pair of hijacked planes sent the twin towers crashing to the ground, the last standing girder was taken down.

With the slice of a magnesium torch, construction workers dismantled the final vestige of the World Trade Center and marked an unofficial end to one of the world's biggest and most heartbreaking recovery efforts.

Mayor Bloomberg, Gov. Pataki and Fire Commissioner Nicholas Scoppetta joined the cops and firefighters, the hardhats and volunteers who descended seven stories into The Pit and watched the beam go down just before 8:30 p.m.

"The construction workers who have dedicated themselves to this effort are on the verge of completing an enormous job, and in many ways this is their night to reflect and remember," Bloomberg said.

The 36-foot-tall, 58-ton column was carefully lifted onto a flatbed truck, where it was covered in a black shroud and secured with black chains before an American flag was draped over it.

At the controls of the crane was Dick Nolan, who helped build the towers three decades ago. "I didn't enjoy this," he said. "But I feel privileged to be lifting out the last piece of steel."

After bagpipers played "Amazing Grace," there was a moment of silence with workers solemnly holding their hardhats over their hearts. As the workers slowly walked up the ramp out of The Pit, they were saluted by firefighters and cops.

Armed services representatives handed the workers folded American flags. Bloomberg, who stood at the top of the ramp, shook every worker's hand.

"Thank you, thank you so much," the mayor said.

Column 1001 B, which had once helped support the southwest corner of the south tower, will be taken to a hangar at Kennedy Airport. One day, it

will be part of a memorial for the more than 2,800 people who died Sept. 11.

After the buildings were destroyed, the rusting beam stood like a steel sentinel amid the devastation and came to symbolize for many the defiance of New Yorkers in the face of terror.

On it, Port Authority police and the city's Finest and Bravest marked their losses in spray paint. At the very top they wrote "PAPD" and the number 37. Then they wrote "NYPD" and the number 23, followed by "FDNY" and the number 343.

"When we came down here this looked insurmountable," Brooklyn iron worker Chris Pillai said. "This is a great tribute to the trades getting together and finishing a monumental task."

LEFT:
Port Authority police,
NYPD and FDNY have
marked their losses on the
last girder standing at
Ground Zero.
James Keivom

RIGHT:
Ironworker Chris Pillai
removes the American flag
from atop the last steel
girder shortly before it is
cut down.
James Keivom

WE WILL NEVER FORGE

Debbie Egan-Chin

Solemn and Silent— Painful Task Ends at Ground Zero

Police and firefighters line the ramp and salute as a flatbed truck carries the flag-covered last girder slowly up from The Pit in a solemn 29-minute ceremony marking the symbolic end of recovery efforts at the site.
Mike Albans

BY GREG GITTRICH AND DAVID SALTONSTALL

Not a word was uttered.

It was a day of quiet dignity and somber pageantry as New York marked the symbolic end of the biggest, most wrenching recovery effort in the nation's history with a simple 29-minute ceremony at Ground Zero.

Nearly nine months after terrorists slammed fuel-laden jets into the World Trade Center—murdering more than 2,800—a solemn honor guard carried a single, flag-draped stretcher out of the yawning pit to mark the 1,730 never found.

Behind this sad procession, strapped to a rumbling flatbed with black chains, came a single, 36-foot-long girder—the last of some 1.6 million tons of twisted steel and concrete removed from the once-towering debris field.

Among those leading the way was Joseph Pfeifer, the first FDNY chief on the scene after the hijacked planes knifed into the twin towers on Sept. 11. His brother, Kevin, an FDNY lieutenant, passed him as he climbed the tower's stairs, but he never came back down.

LEFT:
Firefighters, police officers and victims' families salute
their fallen comrades and loved ones at a solemn
ceremony on the last official day of recovery efforts at
Ground Zero.
Todd Maisel

RIGHT:
An empty, flag-covered stretcher, representing the
1,730 people never found, is carried from the Pit to a
waiting ambulance.
Todd Maisel

His body was not found until February. "Four
months ago, I carried my brother out," said Pfeifer.
"Today, I had the same feeling."

The ceremony was mostly about the victims'
families, who came bearing what tokens they had
— wedding photos, a tattered fire helmet or
banners like the one written in a child's hand that
said, "I love you Daddy sooo much and miss you
sooo much."

"Today is a day to remember those we lost, and
honor those who worked so hard," said mayor
Bloomberg, who organized the ceremony and
insisted that silence, not speeches, would be the
order of the day.

"We will make sure that people, not just in New
York, but in America, never forget what happened
here," Governor Pataki said.

After the bells tolled, the stretcher began its long
march from the far side of Ground Zero. The
girder, led by the mournful thumps of a pipe and
drum unit, followed.

A huge wreath of red, white and blue flowers—as
big around as one of the truck's tires—lay atop the
beam as it was borne up the 515-foot ramp leading
from the base of The Pit.

Taps was played. Five Police Department helicop-
ters, in a V-formation, flew diagonally across the
site. Then bagpipers skirled "America the Beautiful" as the last of the workers headed up the ramp.

The procession then rolled out of The Pit and
turned onto West St., into the loving arms of a
waiting city. Standing shoulder to shoulder, two to
three deep, about 12,500 people lined the 15-block
route. Some bowed their heads. Others cried. Then
everyone began to applaud as the procession eased
by.

"We have to move on now," said Pia Hofmann, a
grapple operator who unearthed many bodies and
was chosen to walk the route beside the ambulance.
"Is it going to be easy? No. But we have to."

Firefighters honor their brothers who were lost in the Sept. 11 attacks.
David Handschuh

An ambulance bearing an empty, flag-covered stretcher, representing the people never found, makes its way slowly up the ramp leading from Ground Zero.
Mike Albans

LEFT:
The last girder from the twin towers is covered by an American flag and
a huge wreath of red, white and blue flowers as a flatbed truck
removes it from the site. The girder was taken to Kennedy Airport to
be stored until it can be used as part of a permanent memorial to the
victims.

ABOVE:
A firefighter consoles a distraught construction worker
following the ceremony.
Michael Appleton

Susan Watts

Acknowledgments

For more photographs of New York, Washington, and the World Trade Center tragedy, visit our photo website, www.DailyNewsPix.com, the world's largest online searchable photo database. Guests can browse through photo galleries as well as do their own searches.

The *Daily News* Photo Archive is the best visual history of 20th century New York in existence. It consists of current color photographs as well as historic black and white images chosen from more than 6 million prints and negatives in the *Daily News* Library. The collection includes staff material that goes back to the paper's founding in 1919 and other material dating back to 1880. The website is updated nightly.

The era of the tabloid newspaper, distinguished by the prominent role played by photographs, began in 1919 with the founding of the New York *Daily News*. The *News* picture collection represents an important piece of modern photojournalistic history, documenting the birth of tabloid photography with its reliance on dynamic images meant to grab the attention and imagination of busy city readers.

Eric Meskauskas
Director of Photography
New York *Daily News*

Staff Photographers
Mike Albans
Willie Anderson
Pat Carroll
Linda Cataffo
Richard Corkery
Harry Hamburg
David Handschuh
James Keivom
Todd Maisel
Thomas Monaster
Ken Murray
John Roca
Robert Rosamilio
Linda Rosier
Andrew Savulich
Howard Simmons
Corey Sipkin
Keith Torrie
Bill Turnbull
Susan Watts
Budd Williams

Contributing Photographers
Ron Antonelli
Michael Appleton
Kristen Artz
KeithBedford
Michael Berman
David Burns
Dennis Clark
Joe DeMaria
Debbie Egan-Chin
Tara Engberg
Dan Farrell
Chet Gordon
Marc Hermann
Georgie Hollingshead
Melissa Jones
Rebecca McAlpin
Bill Miller
Heidi Schumann
Michael Schwartz
Edwine Seymour
Craig Warga

Deputy Director of Photography
Michael Lipack

Photography Editors
Jo Barefoot
Mark Bonifacio
Lee Clark
Carole Lee
Dolores Morrison
Shawn O'Sullivan
Nikhil Rele
Tony Rollo
Charles Ruppmann
Bill Stahl, Jr.
Angela Troisi

Photo Imaging Specialists
Raymond Cruz
Gardy Delatour
Sarah Feinsmith
Marc Grossberg
Lawrence Lai
Ann Marie Linden
Mike Nazario
Rita Robinson
Lloyd Villas